CANADA GEESE

CANADA GEESE

words by JACK DENTON SCOTT

photographs by OZZIE SWEET

G.P. Putnam's Sons | New York

Library of Congress Cataloging in Publication Data
Scott, Jack Denton, 1915-
Canada geese
1. Canada goose—Pictorial works. 2. Birds—North America—Pictorial works
I. Sweet, Ozzie. II. Title.
QL696.A52S34 1976 598.4'1 76-871 SBN 399-20492-X SBN 399-60982-2

Printed in the United States of America
Designed by Bobye List
All Ages

I N THE DARK OF A LATE OCTOBER MOON, IN THE
far north of Canada, geese begin to wing across the cold face
of the sky. Beneath them the grass in the vast marshlands stands
stiff. The tundra is slicked with the soft silver sheen of frost, and
the waters of James Bay and Hudson Bay, capped with waves
stirred up by winds of coming winter, gleam in the moonglow.

The mighty migrations of Canada geese, some 3,000,000 strong,
have begun. They are leaving their breeding grounds in this
northernmost land uninhabited by man to fly south to warmer
temperatures.

6)   The birds burst from the marshes singly and in groups, the flights at the beginning seemingly without pattern. But as they gain altitude, the straggling lines of geese begin to straighten. At first, it looks like a single line of birds, with one flying faster, becoming the leader. But that follow-the-leader group slowly shapes into a loose V outline, the birds churning closer together, as if obeying commands from a flight leader.

High now (probably 3,000 feet, but sometimes as high as 9,000 feet), dark shapes moving away from the moon, the flight of geese looks like a squadron of aircraft flying in tight formation. The V is precise, the point, one bird, the leader, the others spaced evenly behind. It is as perfectly formed as the head of an arrow.

Many of us have watched and listened to migrating geese in the sky. As they speed south, we know that winter is on its way.

8)   We have wondered why the flocks fly in that tight V formation. And is the leader always a wise old bird that knows the way south? Science does not have all the answers, but it does have some.

It is believed that the lead bird, the one at the extreme point of the V, breaks up the air directly ahead, creating updrafts with the tips of its wings. The birds following take advantage of these updrafts by flying slightly to the outside of the bird in front of it. This way the flock can increase its flight range by 70 percent. The air to the side of a flying bird is less turbulent than the air ahead. One bird flying directly behind another would be similar to someone trying to swim behind a motorboat. The alignment or V formation of the birds also permits each bird to see ahead and avoid hazards. Thus the whole flock is not entirely dependent on the leader.

The lead bird is not necessarily a wise old gander that knows the route south. And it does not make the entire flight as the leader. Leaders are changed often and may be a female goose or a gander. Positions are switched because the lead bird breaking the air waves tires more quickly than those following. The V, however, remains as perfect as the birds can make it. In their fixed flight positions, there is no misalignment on the updrafts and flying is easier.

The sounds of migrating Canada geese are as stirring as the sight of them. Each of us has our own reactions, referring to their sounds as honking, calling, or crying. They have been described in various ways: a cry of wildness; an exultant scream of freedom; one of the last pure wild sounds left in a world overwhelmed by civilization. There is nostalgia in it. And poetry. The Cree Indians of the Hudson Bay region call these Canada geese barking across the sky the hounds of heaven.

Canada geese going south flap across the northern two-thirds of America with the speed and accuracy of an arrow, perhaps faster. The birds consistently fly at 40 miles an hour and sometimes, to try to evade bad weather, at 60.

10)   That ageless and mysterious ability of migrating birds to reach their destination accurately and on time through dark of night, buffeting headwinds, fog, and storm still baffles natural scientists. Like some other animals and birds, Canada geese seem to be born with a built-in biological clock, which among other functions signals them when to migrate south, when to return north, and how long to remain at resting stops along the way.

It is easy to understand why geese depart the far north before winter freezes their food sources in the marshlands and ices over the water. Or why they return for late-spring breeding to the isolation of the north, where they can raise their young in safety. But many of the other factors of migration remain puzzling.

Year after year geese return to the exact places in their southern wintering grounds and their northern breeding areas. This phenomenon of migration has long intrigued biologists, but it is only within the last ten years that they have been able to answer even a few of the questions.

It is obvious that it is the goose's combined skills as a meteorologist and a navigator that enables it to travel with almost pinpoint accuracy. But how do birds select direction? Do they know when they have been blown off course? Can they then correct that course? How do they know when they arrive at the exact latitude of their destination?

Today answers are still few, but science concludes that Canada geese migrate by the use of the stars and the sun, the position of the sunset, the direction of the winds in the sky, the direction of the earth's magnetic field, and perhaps also landmarks and the activities and calls of other geese which help them stay on course.

Studies conducted to find the answers are almost as fascinating as the migration itself. Birds are marked with leg tags so that migratory paths and destinations can be plotted when the tagged birds complete their journeys. Geese have been tracked by radar and followed by airplane. They have even been "bugged" by having tiny radio transmitters attached so that they can be tracked electronically.

Some investigators believe that migrating birds are born with an inherited star map which is passed along in the genes from their parents. This means that the birds are born imprinted with a route which follows the stars.

This theory of inheritance was tested by banding some young wildfowl and releasing them long after the parent birds had left for the south. Until this experiment it was believed that the young merely followed the adults along the migratory trail. The theory was exploded when the banded young wildfowl turned up at the wintering grounds. Without guidance or experience, they had flown over unfamiliar territory straight to where their parents were. How? Was that route inherited through their genes? Did they really have a star map imprinted on them at birth?

The star map theory was tested by placing migrating birds in a planetarium. The birds were immediately able to orient themselves by the man-made stars on the planetarium ceiling which duplicated the natural star formation the birds would see on their migratory path. That study, called the Stellar-Orientation System, found that migrating birds relied on the northern circumpolar stars, a grouping of stars in our skies, not only during spring migration, but in the fall.

Migration is much more involved. There are no pat answers, no matter how many studies we do. But we do know that migrating birds are extremely sensitive to minute changes in air pressure and that they may get navigational or directional information from pressure patterns in the earth's atmosphere.

Tests also showed that geese may get some directional information from the earth's magnetic field. We do not know for certain, but it is possible they have an organ in their physical makeup that responds to the directional pull of the magnetic field of the earth, much as the needle in a compass points to show direction. But much of this is still scientific guesswork, and the geese still go their unerring way without leaving many telltale clues of how they make their remarkable passage.

Although the method of migration may be uncertain, the route is clear. Canada geese use four flyways: the Atlantic, the Mississippi, the Central, the Pacific. During the migrations south and the return north in spring these four flyways are as busy as superhighways.

The geese we watched fly across the moon are using the Mississippi Flyway. They are a certain kind of goose, the Todd's Canada, which can weigh more than 10 pounds and are probably the most numerous and popular of the large family which numbers ten other subspecies, ranging from the 2½- to the 4-pound cackling Canada, to the giant Canada, which weighs as much as 20 pounds. This regal bird was thought to be extinct fifty years ago but was rediscovered near Rochester, Minnesota, in 1960 and is again thriving. The others in the Canada clan are the Richardson's, Taverner's, Aleutian, Lesser Canada, Vancouver, Dusky, Atlantic, and the Western.

This flock of Todd's from northern Canada numbers several hundred birds, consisting of dozens of families and their offspring. There is no tail wind this moonlit night as they fly toward their first destination. If there were, the wind would push them into a 70-mile-an-hour speed and bring them in just twelve hours nonstop to where they will feed and rest for several days. Each goose needs one-half pound of food a day, and migrating birds need more than this to fuel their passage. Thus, the flock will make rest-and-food stops along the way before setting down for their short stay in Wisconsin.

A female leads the flock. She and the other geese are in deadly danger as she guides them to their first stop. As they approach civilization, they face a danger worse than a crippling storm or a hurricane. This danger, the Canada goose's only important enemy, waits in every state for the birds to drop out of the sky for rest and food. It tempts them to come down and land at specific places.

14)   The enemy does this in clever ways. Migrating geese often will stop if they see other geese feeding safely in a field below. They also will land at cornfields where the reaper has been through, leaving some ears on the ground. And they are tempted to stop and rest if they see an open pond or other small body of water beside a meadow where they can graze on the grass, then drink the water that they need. They are almost sure to stop if they see other migrating geese resting safely on the water.

So sometimes the enemy puts its "geese" there. They aren't real geese, but skillfully made of papier-mâché or plastic or carved from wood, they look exactly like Canada geese.

Not far from these enticing decoys the hunters wait, hidden in blinds, shotguns ready. If the geese hesitate to land, seem nervous, unsure, some of these hunters are also adept at calling the Canadas in, cleverly imitating the welcoming and assembly calls.

Canada geese are among the most intelligent of all birds, but when migrating, they are hungry and tired, a combination that dulls their wariness.

Now, as they speed south in early-morning sunlight, 3,000 feet up, the leader of the flock spots an ideal landing situation, an open meadow, a large cornfield, and, sparkling in the distance, a pond.

She brakes, flares, waggles her wings, sending the signal back through the flock. The large compact V flight halts its forward drive, all wings seeming to churn in unison. Then they follow their leader as she loses altitude, sets her wings, lowers her feet, which are her landing gear. The younger and less experienced birds, constituting one-third of the flock, honk loudly as they bank, eager to land and feed. Their tumult, as usual, alerts the wary leader. She flares back into the sky, making a wide, high circle, double-checking for danger that the noise of the young geese may have brought into the open. The flock follows. The fields lie silent and tempting below. Assured, the leader again sets her wings and makes her descent. She is weary now from buffeting the airwaves. She will be content to feed and let a new leader take them farther south.

The flock is not organized as it comes down out of the sky. Birds are everywhere, each goose setting its wings, gliding, feet down, searching for a safe landing area.

16) Some are almost in the field when the hunters open fire. The female leader is the first to fall; then others all around her crumple to the ground, wings outstretched, still beating helplessly.

Crying and frantically flailing their wings to gain altitude and escape, the rest of the flock is now in a state of panic as the gunfire continues and birds plummet from the sky.

Finally, the geese are high enough, out of reach of the powerful shotguns below. Four thousand feet up the flock regroups. The mate of the female leader that was killed takes command, guiding the flight, now re-forming into its V, higher, higher, until the fleeing geese look like the tattered remnants of a cloud.

No one can tell us what that lead goose feels or if he has the capacity for sorrow. But the goose that was killed was this gander's lifetime mate, and his cry as he guides his flock south sounds piercing and mournful.

The conservationists, biologists, and other experts, however, do not decry this scene that we have just witnessed. They say that for the three million geese migrating south there is only enough food in their wintering grounds to feed half that number. In their view, controlled hunting is humane because it prevents starvation and keeps existing flocks healthy. But many of us wonder about this logic when we witness geese that have been wounded and crippled, their death and suffering delayed. But perhaps death by gun that also puts food on our table is preferable to geese becoming diseased through poor health or starving because there is not enough food for all of them.

The balance of nature is a complicated matter. Man sometimes steps in to even the scales, especially when the imbalance has been of his own making. The whitetail deer would not have survived in this country if it had not been for the careful harvesting of these overpopulated deer by hunters. But the deer actually became overpopulated because its natural predators such as the mountain lion and the wolf had been almost wiped out by man.

The Canada geese, however, do not have to face the hunters' guns throughout their journey. All over the country are National Wildlife Refuges, where hunting is prohibited by national and state law. Well spaced along the flyways are huge areas containing lakes and vast marshlands that offer safety and food.

The new leader of this flight is taking his followers to such a refuge, Horicon Marsh in east-central Wisconsin. This four-year-old gander has been here every year of his life, and so have many other members of the flock.

This time, as they approach the refuge, there is no cautious circling or nervous maneuvering. Geese are everywhere, in the air, on the water, in the marshland. The flights are slow, peaceful. The birds sit calmly on the water, some of them lifting their heads and watching newcomers arrive, much like people at a camp or trailer park taking a look at the late arrivals.

The flight of Todds breaks into segments as it arrives, tired *(19* geese setting their wings and gliding on the water. Having lost about 10 percent of their body weight during the flight some go directly to the grass for food. As the flock settles down, other flights continue to arrive, V wedges high in the sky, as wave after wave of 150,000 Canada geese come to this Wisconsin place of refuge.

Here they laze and feed for indefinite periods, but they will all eventually head farther south to the place where they have always gone to winter. As dusk seeps its soothing violet light over the Horicon Marsh, perhaps a week after the flight of Todds arrived, those families that joined in forming that V in the moonlight over Canada slowly begin to take off from the protected marshland. Stark against the darkening skyline, they begin their seven-hour nonstop flight to their wintering grounds in that broad region where the Ohio River joins the Mississippi River. There they will make their usual choice of six large refuges in the states that border that area, Illinois, Missouri, Kentucky, and Tennessee. They will be joined by other Canada geese that migrated through Michigan, Ohio, and Indiana and help complete the Mississippi Valley goose population.

The wintering grounds are also the ancient mating grounds. Here mates who will remain lifetime partners are chosen.

The gander that lost his mate to hunters moves carefully among his flock searching for a female. A large, strong bird weighing 11 pounds, he is experienced, knows what he is looking for, and will fight to win the female that appeals to him. No one but a gander knows the features a gander looks for in a female, but it takes this particular male three days to choose a new mate. She is a three-year-old, ready to mate, and he finds her standing with another female at the edge of the water in marsh grass.

He carefully reaches over and touches her bill with his, as she demurely lowers her head. When the gander turns, he finds another male on the water four feet away, glaring at him, raising his wings. As the other bird belligerently swims to shore, without hesitation, the gander lowers his head, stretching it straight out, spearlike, and rushes the other bird, knocking it back into the water. At the same time he raises his wings and flails the other male, hitting him hard with the bony outer edge of both wings.

It is not much of a fight, although if the other male had the strength and experience of the older gander, it could continue for as long as a half hour. But this time the younger bird senses superiority and flies across the water, making it no contest. The victorious gander honks loudly, makes a series of snoring sounds, and approaches the female. He positions his neck close to the ground, weaving it snakelike, opening his bill, distending his feathers, rustling them, and, as he gets closer, hisses at her,

Watching him approach, she also lowers her neck, fluffs her feathers, opens her bill, but stands still as he comes close, brushing gently against her. The male turns and walks away. She honks loudly and follows him across the shoreline as he moves slowly in a stately strut.

Suddenly he takes off, flying across the marshland. She follows close behind, and from now on wherever he goes she will follow. If he naps on the water close to marsh grass, she snuggles up beside him. They are paired, an inseparable team that will stay together for as long as they both live. Geese have been known to give their lives for each other if need be. One Canada gander knocked a man from horseback as he came too close to his mate, killing himself with the force of the blow that tumbled the 200-pound man from the saddle.

Life in the wintering grounds is relaxed. Long periods are spent grooming those distinctive feathers that make the Canada goose unlike any other bird. Head and neck are a shining black, broken by an oval patch of white, running from the upper side of the head down each cheek and necklacing under the throat. That long black neck contrasts starkly with the pale-gray chest and gray-brown body and wings. Belly and flanks are white; upper and lower tail coverts, covering the black rump feathers, are white. The average gander weighs anywhere from 8 to 12 pounds, with the goose 2 to 3 pounds lighter. Other than this, they are identical. The adult Todd gander's body is from 34 to 40 inches in length, and the wing-spread 5 and sometimes as much as 6 feet.

That frequent preening of feathers is not vanity. It is an important function that keeps the goose flying. With its bill, the bird collects oil from a preen gland, the uropygial, at the base of the tail. That oil consisting of fatty acid, fat, and wax is gathered on the bill, then carefully worked into and onto the feathers.

It both waterproofs and prevents the feathers from fraying and becoming dry. And it conditions and lubricates the bill itself. Places the bill cannot reach, such as the head and throat, are oiled by the bird rubbing its head on the oil gland, then on the feathers. Without oiling, feathers would be dry, function poorly, and be as useless as an automobile without oil.

Healthy, well-oiled feathers are light, waterproof, and warm. The surface or contour feathers overlap like shingles on a roof and shed moisture easily. The important flight feathers at the edge of the outer wing are light, strong, and as flexible as wire.

Underneath the contour feathers is a thick layer of down, a tufted covering without the shafts of feathers, which creates a dead air space that acts as an excellent insulator. On wintry days the geese fluff their feathers to increase that air space and conserve heat. In summer they tighten them to keep the heat out. Biologists claim that a Canada goose has 12,000 skin muscles, which give the bird marvelous feather control.

Even the Canada's legs set the bird apart from other waterfowl. They are closer to the center of the goose's body than those of ducks or swans. This gives the Canada excellent balance and enables it to walk better than most other water birds. When they can walk, rather than fly, often they do, sometimes for long distances. In the safety of refuges or in the northern marshlands they walk much more than they fly. The black feet, which are covered with scales, have four toes. Three point forward and are connected by two webs that reach to the toe. The fourth toe, which points backward, is smaller and free from the web. The goose walks on its toes. In swimming the toes fold together when the foot pushes forward, so there is little resistance. But on the backward paddle the toes spread apart, pushing the wide webs against the water and propelling the goose rapidly ahead.

Tip-up feeding, with the tip of the tail straight up and head underwater, is a method of reaching for marine growth, sago, pondweed, eel or widgeon grass, or sea lettuce, with balance maintained by vigorous paddling with those webbed feet. The Canada skillfully probes the bottom with the bill, which is so sensitive that it selects and rejects without the goose having to yank the food object to the surface to inspect it.

That black bill is high at the base, narrows in the middle, and tapers toward the end. Its edges, which are serrated, act as a strainer. The front is the cutter that clips the grasses and plants and, aided by powerful jaw muscles, strips kernels from ears of corn. The tip is extremely sensitive; 2,000 tactile corpuscles are connected to nerve endings. That horny-hard bill is used as a weapon, as a working tool for building nests, for grooming and oiling the feathers, and as an aid in communication, funneling sound from the trachea or windpipe.

Canada geese seem to "talk" constantly, the sounds of a flock on water not unlike those of people at a large party, running from chatterings, snorts, grunts, murmurings, coughs, squawks to hisses and honkings.

Scientists Lawrence Jahn and Nicholas Collias, studying a flock of Canadas at length, discovered that there are ten distinct vocalizations, each one seemingly a response to another sound. Here, as reported by writer and goose student Joe Van Wormer, is a table of goose talk.

1. Hissing, used for threat and alarm.

2. Honking, hornlike, it is blast-loud and warns and claims territory; it calls and answers mates; it is an alarm, is used as a greeting when geese return and just before takeoff and during flight.

3. One mate calling another at short distance, sounding like *come, come, come,* uttering one call a second repeatedly.

4. Call to goslings, like the above, only sharper.

5. Gander's special call to mate, loud snoring sound.

6. Post-copulation call, a quick snore.

7. Scream. Usually of pain when a bird is bitten by another.

8. Distress call, very loud, *oh!-oo, oh!oo,* made by mates that are separated or geese attacked by others.

9. Goslings' call of distress, loud, continual *peep, peep, peep,* usually given when the young are lost or confused.

10. Contentment calls of goslings, soft, *wheeoo, wheeoo,* repeated.

The scientists do not mention the very distinct barking sound of the Canadas when they are flying and nearly always when they are migrating.

Brown irises and black pupils characterize the enormous eyes of Canadas, and their eyesight, far superior to people's, is superb. With eyes on the side of the head, vision is monocular, or one-sided, but since the eyes are close to the top of the head, they also have a range of nearly three-quarters of a circle horizontally. In comparison, we can see less than 180 degrees horizontally and only slightly on each side, unless we move our heads. Directly ahead geese also have binocular vision, as we do. Although its eyes are not as moveable as ours, the goose can turn its head and take in overhead, front, and sides quickly, something we cannot do. The ears, invisible under the feathers, are located on the side of the head, approximately where ours are, and hearing is as keen as eyesight. The only sense that is not finely developed is smell, and that does not seem to be a detriment.

Although Canadas are social birds and rarely mingle with any but their own kind, within the large gatherings of geese there are distinct groupings. Mates are fiercely loyal to each other and their families and are not interested in geese other than their own. The larger the family, the greater the status of that family. Social scale and pecking order work down from that. Thus, the boss gander has the largest family. The next most important gander has the second largest family, working down to the small family, then to the pair of birds just mated. The single unattached bird is at the bottom of the status ladder. Canadas treat unattached geese with suspicion.

The most important gander's family grows through his ability as a producer and includes not only his own offspring, but his children's children and in-laws as well. Even after the Canadas' young are mated and their offspring have offspring, the family groups get together. Grandmother geese are as protective of grand-goslings as they are of their current hatch.

36) The most important occupation during the wintering south is constant feeding. The Canadas seem to know that they must build up reserves of subcutaneous fat (the fat under the skin) to take them on the long journey northward again. So, although they laze and preen and feed on water plants, grazing is their main feeding activity. They like many varieties of grass and grains, but their preference is for the young green shoots of all plant life. Cornfields are also favorites.

Without warning large flocks take off from the water of their wintering grounds, gaggles of geese flapping away, the flights without form or regimen, the winging slow, undulating. Even so, as they rise higher into the sky, the families edge toward one another, and by the time they arrive at the feeding grounds they have grouped with their own gander.

The gander head of each family leads the way down from the sky
into the feeding area, but each goose is its own flight master and
carefully selects the landing site. Thus, the flight seems to hang
against the sky as if painted there, each bird hovering, wings
spread wide in a glide, tails fanned, feet down. On the ground, as
usual, families stay together.

An ideal feeding area is one that provides both grass and grain. Meadows bordering cornfields are the target of the geese here. As they feed, each family depends on two birds to act as sentinels. Some sort of silent signal by the gander designates the sentinels. They stand alert, heads moving like radar horn antennae, which, with the geese's vision and hearing, are about as effective as radar for their purpose. Strange sights and sounds that they cannot identify will bring warning cries, and the flock will immediately take to the air. But with the Canada's high intelligence, there are no idle warnings, and sentinels are never skittery, uncertain, or nervous. Geese know their friends and enemies. Dogs bother them; so do men. Cars, aircraft, and most wild animals do not.

If we could watch this flock feed throughout the day, we would see the changing of the guard, the sentinels being relieved so they can feed. Again, it is done by that signal known only to the geese.

sentinel

sentinel

Goats cannot crop grass any closer. Blades of grass are nipped with the front of that versatile bill, and a quick jerk of the head backward enables the cutting edge of the bill to slice the grass off neatly as a knife.

Often the flock will stay in the pastures, meadows, and cornfields late and not arrive back at their settlement and water site until moonrise.

This is the pattern of their winter months, peaceful feeding in fields, long, relaxed sessions in marshlands and on water, lazy, unhurried flights. If geese have such a period as a vacation, this is it.

Sometime late in March, as dusk begins to darken the skyline, the gander with his new mate behind him takes to the air. The exodus north begins. He is pushed by that timeless urge to reproduce and will breed only in the far north, where he himself was born.

This time there are no straggling lines. The gander immediately takes the lead, and the V of long flight is quickly formed.

But this flight is unhurried, almost leisurely. The Canadas' mysterious time clock tells them that to rush back to their north-land would bring them there too early, and the ice and snow would still be there. There are many stops for food and rest. Some stops are in the wild places where elk graze. But now that the hunting season is closed, there is no danger from guns, and the Canadas seem to know it. People and their civilization appear to offer no threats.

The geese land in fields close to farms. They pick up grit, small stones, beside busy highways. The grit helps the gizzard, a small, compact organ that softens and crushes food, grind up the grass and stubble that they eat. The calm, unhurried birds ignore the cars speeding by.

Although the geese seem oblivious to the sounds (which would send them flying in the fall) in the nearby farm, they still search for corn spilled during harvesting in a field. They try to feed well at every stop, as if knowing that they must arrive in the northland in excellent condition. For despite their excellent timing, sometimes after they arrive there, even in late spring, freak weather will bring bitter cold and snow, and without the reserves of fat built up along the way they could perish.

But the migrating Canadas dally only so long. Their superb time clock finally sends them speeding nonstop into the wilderness where they were born. That last leg of the flight to the ancient breeding grounds in the immense Canadian marshes that extend almost to the Arctic coast is a long one.

Arriving tired, resting on the water even before looking for food,

the geese would be much more tired if it weren't for special air
sacs in their bone structure which connect with chambers throughout their bodies. On long flights such as this last one, the wing
muscles create much heat, which would be exhausting and harmful,
if these air sacs weren't there to help the lungs pump in oxygen
and lower body temperature.

Despite the long flight, the urge to reproduce and give birth to young that will carry on the species is so strong that the gander soon takes his new mate on a nest-site tour.

The nest must not only have a solid foundation, isolation, and good visibility, but it must be near open water, have a close cover of high grass or plants and a grass browsing area for the goslings.

After they find a suitable place, the gander and his goose mate physically. The action is on the water, with the female partly submerged. It is ritualistic, with one or both birds dipping heads into the water and spraying it over their backs.

After the breeding they raise their heads, point their bills skyward, then spin about and face each other, the gander making his snorting or snoring sounds.

Soon the goose builds her nest, fashioning it from marsh grass,
twigs, and branches and pulling down from her breast to give it a
soft, warm lining. The nest is 5 inches deep, with an inside diame-
ter of 10 inches, an outside one of 40 inches.

In less than an hour after the nest is built she lays the first egg.
After that an egg appears about every one and one-half days, with
a total of from two to nine dull white eggs. This spring she will lay
five eggs, but only four will hatch. After laying each egg, she pulls
more down from her breast, and more during incubation, creating
a bare spot, referred to as the incubation patch because she holds
this bare skin against the eggs to keep them at an even temperature.

During this period the gander remains on guard close by. He threatens any intruder, including other geese, by stretching almost flat on the water, pointing his lowered head and hissing angrily.

Unlike some other birds, whose nest duty is shared by the male, the goose does all the incubating, which may take from twenty-five to twenty-eight days, with the gander always close by. She leaves the nest for brief intervals for food and water and regularly turns the eggs to give them an even temperature. Not only does this careful turning give all the eggs the same heat, but it prevents the membrane enclosing the chick within one egg from sticking to the shell.

The goose is vulnerable as she spends almost a month on the nest, but only a very large predator such as a coyote would dare face a pair of brave and determined Canadas. If danger threatens, the goose squats low on her nest and lays her head and neck flat on the ground. Her soft gray and black coloring is excellent camouflage, blending her in with the shadows.

She defends her nest with vigor. The naturalist John James Audubon nearly had an arm broken when he got too close to a nesting goose. She flipped out a knobby wing with such power that he couldn't use his arm for a week.

Two days before hatching, peeping sounds come from the eggs. Inside the egg, each unborn gosling has a sharp egg tooth on the tip of its tiny black bill. Even after the first crack in the eggshell is made by that tooth, it can take the gosling two long, grueling days to break its way through.

It emerges gradually, slick, wet feathers helping it slide out of the shell. Twenty-four hours after the first baby goose breaks the egg barrier four are hatched.

The goose carefully hovers over them for twenty-four hours until they are dry and downy. This is the most important period of their life. Now they become imprinted. Both goose and gander stand close to the nest so the goslings recognize them as their parents, and the young will also know that they, too, are geese. For geese, unlike most other birds and animals, are not born knowing what they are. Newborn goslings (incubated by artificial means) that saw a man or a horse first adopted them as their parents. A famous case was of naturalist Konrad Lorenz becoming father to an entire clutch of goslings that followed him everywhere, even when they were adult birds.

The yellow and olive downy little geese are fortunate. Besides being perky and handsome, they are precocial, which means they can be independent right away: Eyes are open at birth; they can run as soon as they are dry, and soon after hatching, they can leave the nest and join the mother and father in hunting for food. Once the goose and her brood leave the nest they never return to it.

The gander leads the way to the new life, the goose bringing up
the rear, as they keep the goslings between them. They slowly swim
around, introducing the little geese to their environment.

The four goslings double their weight in a week. They learn their life-style by copying the actions of their parents, who teach them tip-up diving and what food to look for.

60)   The goslings have many enemies—predatory birds, large turtles, even herons. But a day-old gosling can dive and swim forty feet underwater, and these four always have at least one parent with them to beat off most predators.

In two weeks the goslings become gray and weigh one pound.
Feathers begin to appear. In a month they weigh four pounds.
They still retain some down, but now the feathers are sprouting
all over. In six weeks color appears, the white cheek patches begin
to show, as do the black feathers.

By the time these four are two months old they weigh twenty-
four times what they did at birth. At this point they can eat their
own weight in food every day. That appetite lessens as they grow
older.

When the goslings are half grown, their parents moult, losing
their flight feathers. During this period they cannot fly. But they
are safe in their far northern retreat.

It takes about ninety-five days for the pair of Canadas to nest, incubate the eggs, and raise their four youngsters to the age when they can fly. The adult moult is also over at this time, and parents and offspring joyously take to the air together.

The female continues to guide and instruct her four goslings, swimming with them everywhere, flying with them when they try their wings.

Leaves fall from the trees colored and brittle by the time the four young geese fly around the marsh by themselves. Nights are crisp; fish seek the mud in the bottom of the lake for their winter hibernation. The moon is hazy, and the grasses in the marshlands begin to stiffen.

The gander and his goose become restless, and so does the rest of the adult flock. They fluff their feathers and fidget on the water and watch clouds scud across the sky.

One night when the October moon is full, moved by that strong migratory urge, the flock suddenly takes to the air, two by two, family by family, honking, wings whistling.

On the far edge of the lake the four goslings that have become geese watch their parents leave their marshland world crying wildly.

64)   Their own honking is shrill and their flight slower as the four
goslings fly through moonlight to join the rapidly forming V
flight. The family groups gather high in the sky, wings churning,
waiting for all of this year's young geese to join them before they
travel south through the night, guided by their star maps.